# Introduction

THE MOST DARING THING A MAN OR WOMAN CAN SAY IS THAT THEY HAVE FOUND GOD. The claim is quite staggering. Yet throughout time millions of people have made it. In our own day and age it is made by thousands of people in every country of the world. They make this claim, not in the sense of 'I *hope* I have found Him', or 'I *think* I have found Him', but 'I *know*'. They are so sure they have found Him that nothing can shake them or move them from that conviction. I dare to suggest that after you have read this booklet, you can find Him too.

For several decades I have been helping people come to know God. The steps they have taken are simple but have brought them into intimate and personal contact with the Creator of the universe. In this booklet, these steps are laid out in a way that is easy to follow. Think of it as a traveller's guide – a stage-by-stage explanation to help you get from where you are to finding God.

Each one of these steps is based on what God has revealed to us about Himself in the Bible. If it were not for the Bible we would know very little about the Creator. That is why, in outlining the steps by which you can find God, I draw heavily upon those parts of the Bible that are appropriate to the task that is before us – finding God. To that task we turn together now.

# Believe He is there!

**STEP 01**

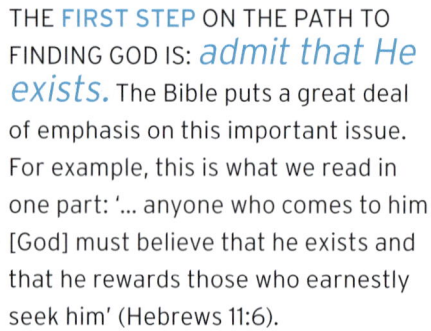

THE FIRST STEP ON THE PATH TO FINDING GOD IS: *admit that He exists.* The Bible puts a great deal of emphasis on this important issue. For example, this is what we read in one part: '... anyone who comes to him [God] must believe that he exists and that he rewards those who earnestly seek him' (Hebrews 11:6).

Clearly we can't expect to find God unless we believe He is there. But how can we be sure that He exists? Throughout time philosophers and great thinkers have spent endless hours debating the issue of whether or not God exists. As a young man I swung between belief and unbelief on this important issue. One day, however, I put aside my prejudice and took a close look at the universe around me. If there is no God, I said to myself, how did universal law and order come into being? By chance?

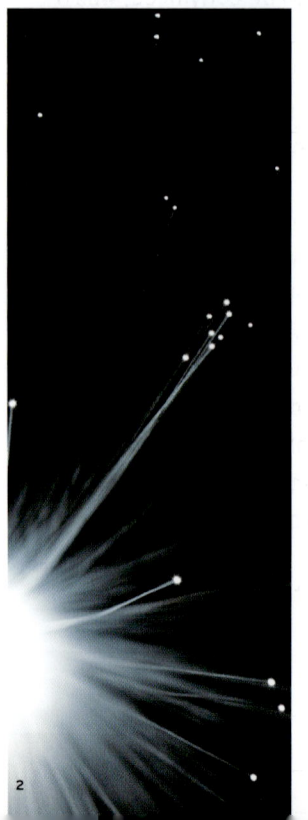

The more I thought about this, the more the idea seemed improbable.

How could a universe such as this, I reasoned, a universe filled with a cosmic orderliness that stretches from the molecule to the most distant star, come together by chance? And how could this orderliness just happen to stay together by chance throughout thousands and thousands of years? That, I came to be convinced, was a hypothesis that stretched credulity. It involved believing that universal chaos gave birth to universal order – *by chance*. Anyone who believed that must spell 'chance' with a capital 'C' and mean by it – God.

I asked a commercial printer once (in the days when type was individual pieces of metal): 'If you were to keep throwing the individual letters up in the air, how long do you think it would take for them to fall and form themselves into one of Wordsworth's poems?' He replied, 'The possibilities of that happening by chance are so remote it is not even worth considering.'

Someone has figured out how many chances to one it would take for the world to have happened by chance, and the figures go round the world thirty-five times. Sir James Jeans, a scientist, worked out that it would take 100 million years for 100,000 monkeys, tapping at random on 100,000 typewriters, to produce by chance one of the plays of Shakespeare. And then, even after the letters had been formed, they wouldn't know what the words meant! When you pick up a book and see there is intelligence in it, you know that behind it is an intelligent mind expressing itself.

# *intelligence*

Look at the universe again – it too responds to intelligence. It can be intelligently studied. Intelligence has gone into it and since that intelligence is so wide and awesome, you have to spell it with a capital 'I' – *Intelligence*. Personally I prefer to use the word *God*. Perhaps you too may come to prefer using that word.

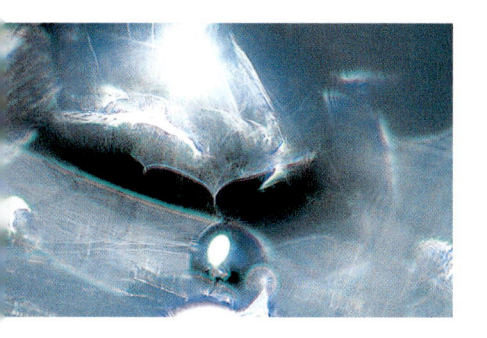

# At home in God

**STEP** 02

THE SECOND STEP TO FINDING GOD IS: *realise that when God created human beings, He designed us to enjoy a close relationship with Himself.*

The apostle Paul, when speaking to a group of people in Athens during the early days of Christianity, said that God had created all men and women so that they would 'seek him ... reach out for him and find him'. Then he added these memorable words: 'For in him we live and move and have our being' (Acts 17:27-28).

Augustine, one of the leaders of the Christian Church in the fourth century, put it like this: 'God has made us for Himself and our hearts are restless until they find their rest in Him.' This restlessness has been described by someone as a 'nostalgia for God'. The word 'nostalgia', I understand, comes from two Greek words – *nostos*, meaning 'return home', and *algos*, meaning 'pain'. It meant originally 'incurable homesickness' – incurable by anything except, of course, *home*. Take it from me – your soul and mine will never get over their restlessness until they find their home in God.

Because of this longing for a relationship with Him that our Creator has built into us, there is a part of us that nothing in this world will ever be able to satisfy. Money will not satisfy it. Fame will not satisfy it.

Pleasure will not satisfy it. Consider carefully this next statement, as it is one of the most important things I have said so far: *there is something in us that cannot be satisfied by our father or mother, our spouse, our family, or our nearest and dearest friend.* What we long for at the core of our souls simply isn't there in any earthly relationship. Understanding this can revolutionise our lives. Not to realise it means that we will go through life seeking to cram into our souls every possible activity we can find in the hope that the ache within us will be satisfied. Then, whenever the things we do fail to produce a deep sense of satisfaction, and the discomfort within us becomes almost unbearable, we set about anaesthetising it with more and more pleasurable activities - another shopping spree, another holiday, another game of golf, another film, and so on. There is nothing wrong with pleasure - legitimate pleasure, that is - but it simply cannot meet the needs of that deep part of our being that we often call the soul. Outside of God there is no relief for the part of our being that aches for Him.

satisfaction

# Our Greatest Sin

**STEP** 03

THE THIRD STEP TO FINDING GOD IS: *face the fact that our greatest sin lies in resisting God's attempts to establish a relationship with us.* When Jesus Christ was here on earth, He once spoke on behalf of God to a group of people and said: 'These are the Scriptures that testify about me, yet you refuse to come to me to have life' (John 5:39-40).

*endence*

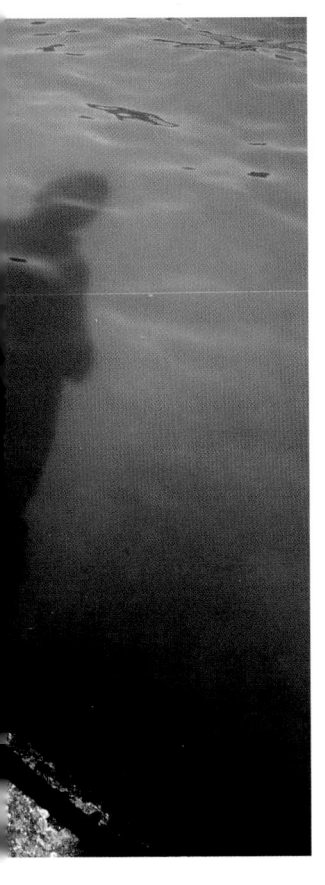

Down the centuries people have debated the question: what is sin? Some list things like murder, adultery, lying, stealing, greed, and so on, as examples of sin. But sin is much deeper than wrong behaviour. It is the *cause* behind wrong behaviour. And that cause is a determination to have our own way no matter what God or anyone else thinks.

The best definition of sin I have ever come across is this: 'a declaration of independence'. Embedded like splintered glass in the centre of our souls is a stubborn commitment to independence. In practical terms it means that when God says, 'I want to come into your life and establish a relationship with you,' there is something in us that rises up and says, 'No, I want to run my life in my own way and on my own terms.' If this spirit of independence is not recognised

*longing*

it will block our way to knowing God, for before anything can be effectively dealt with, it must first be identified.

Our problem in a nutshell is this: God has built within every one of us a longing to know Him and have a relationship with Him, but there is also present in us a strong streak of independence that wants to make our lives work in the way we think best, without having to refer to God. This shows itself in one of two ways. We either deny we have a longing for God, or we go about trying to meet that longing in ways that do not involve Him.

Denial, however, does not work. It not only distances us from the longings God has placed within us for Himself, but it also drives those longings underground, where they produce an intolerable desire for other sources of satisfaction. As I said earlier, nothing can satisfy the desire for God other than God. Better to face reality and deal with the independence that strives to keep us self-sufficient. Independence may seem as nothing when placed alongside such acts as murder, adultery, lying, stealing and so on, but it is the root of sin, nevertheless. If you accept the definition of sin as being 'a declaration of independence', can you see that it is possible to live a life free of all those things I have mentioned, and yet still be guilty of great sin?

**STEP** 04

# A Change of Mind

FOLLOWING ON CLOSELY FROM WHAT I HAVE JUST SAID, THE FOURTH STEP IS THIS: *be willing not only to recognise a spirit of independence in yourself, but also be willing to repent of it.* The apostle Peter, when speaking to a group of people in Jerusalem, put it like this: 'Repent, then, and turn to God, so that your sins may be wiped out …' (Acts 3:19).

turn

The act of turning from living without reference to God is described in the Bible as 'repentance'. The English word comes from the Greek word *metanoia*, which means 'a change of mind'. Basically, repentance is a change of mind about how life works and where true life is to be found. But to understand this matter fully, we need to see that more goes on in repentance than a mental evaluation that we have been moving in the wrong direction and need to follow a new one. It also involves a heartfelt sadness that we have ignored God in our lives for so long.

One very self-willed man came to see how deeply committed he was to living independently of God. After this, he said to me: 'Surely God doesn't want me to squirm over my sin of independence before He establishes a relationship with me?' I replied, 'No, it is not a matter of squirming, but more a matter of seeing how your self-centredness and self-sufficiency have offended the Creator, and being genuinely sorry about that.' He wasn't prepared, as he put it, to 'eat humble pie', and the result was that he didn't, at that point in his life, find God.

Later, I am glad to say, he was able to repent sincerely. When he did, it was the beginning of a wonderful relationship with God which, to the best of my knowledge, he continues to enjoy.

Let me make one thing clear – repentance is not a superficial matter or just a ritual to perform. It is something deeper than eating humble pie. It involves looking away from all unreality, such as denying we have a soul that longs after God, or trying to make our souls come alive apart from Him. It means being willing to recognise the hopelessness of our attempts to try and make life work without recourse to God.

At this moment you may be saying, 'I see the point, but I find it difficult to work up any deep emotion about it'. Don't worry. When you decide to allow God into your life, providing you are sincere in wanting to repent, God will help you enter into the meaning and reality of it. You supply the willingness; He supplies the power.

*repentance*

# No Other Way

**STEP** 05

THE **FIFTH STEP** ON THE WAY TO FINDING GOD IS: *understand that no one can come to God except through His Son, the Lord Jesus Christ.* This is how Christ Himself put it: 'I am the way and the truth and the life. No-one comes to the Father except through me' (John 14:6).

reconcile

If you have ever wondered what Christianity is all about, here's the answer – it is all about Jesus Christ. He is God's Son who came to earth 2,000 years ago, died on a cross, was resurrected from the dead and returned again to heaven. The fact that He came to this earth cannot be disputed. Every time we write the date we attest it. The years are recorded on our calendars as being so many years *after* Christ – AD stands for *anno Domini*, 'in the year of our Lord'. The story of how He entered into human life as a baby in Bethlehem is an amazing miracle. The term used to describe this astonishing event is 'incarnation', which means 'God clothing Himself in human flesh'. We celebrate that event every Christmas.

But let's look a little more closely at why Jesus came. His purpose was twofold – to *reveal* God to us and to *reconcile* us to God. He revealed the true nature of God in the way He went about doing good and working miracles, and He reconciled us to God by His death upon a cross. Maybe you have wondered to yourself: why do Christians make so much of the cross?

It's a vast subject, but let me see if I can put it in a nutshell. God created a good and just universe. It reflected who He is – a holy and just God. He created us so that we could enjoy a close relationship with Him. Then sin came into the world. Your sin and mine (our stubborn commitment to living independently of God) has separated us from Him. In a good and just universe, our sin needs to be atoned for before we can again enjoy a relationship with God. Because of His love for us, God sent His Son Jesus to earth to reveal the Father's love for us. Jesus did this by showing us the way to live and by willingly dying for our sins on the cross. He made the sacrifice required to atone for the sin of the whole world. If we accept and receive the work Jesus did for us on the cross, we can be forgiven and set free to enjoy relationship with God.

# the way

There is no way that we can come to God except through His Son. He is not *a* way, as if there are many others. He is *the* Way, the only way.

Many years ago a missionary was lost in one of Africa's jungles and he asked a local to help him find the way. As the African led the way through the jungle the missionary, seeing no track, became doubtful as to the local's knowledge and said, 'I see no track. Are you sure this is the way?' The local said, 'There is no way. I am the way.' Christians are people who have come to God through Christ – *the* Way.

**STEP** 06

# Count the Cost

WE COME NOW TO THE **SIXTH STEP** TO FINDING GOD: *count the cost.* This is what Jesus told some people when He was here on earth: 'Suppose one of you wants to build a tower. Will he not first sit down and estimate the cost to see if he has enough money to complete it?' (Luke 14:28).

*the cost*

These words are part of a story Jesus told about a man who wanted to put up a building but, before doing so, sat down and carefully thought through all the implications of what he was about to do. In telling this story, Jesus wanted to show that before committing our lives to Him, we ought to think carefully about what is involved. So, before you consider taking the final step, think with me for a moment about what it is going to mean for you to commit yourself to knowing God through His Son, Jesus Christ.

It is going to require (as we have said) an about-turn in your life through a radical act of repentance.

This means turning from the barren sources where you have tried to find life and committing the welfare of your whole being into the hands of God. It also involves opening yourself up to God, asking Him to forgive you and accept you into His family.

Another thing to consider is this - some things might have to go after you have committed your life to Christ. You will need to break, for example, with some things that may have become part of your lifestyle. Lying, cheating, moral impurity and so on, are not consistent with being a follower of Jesus. This does not mean that after you become a Christian you will never fail or fall. But if you do lapse, you will find that you will not want to stay there. And Christ's strength and power will be there to help you find His forgiveness, get up and go on.

Yet another consideration is this - you will need, when appropriate, to identify yourself as a Christian to others. I encourage you not be a *secret* follower of Christ. It costs something to be a follower of Jesus, but the benefits are beyond telling.

Assuming that at this point you are close to being ready to make the decision to turn your life over to God and ask the Lord Jesus Christ into your life, I want to give you one final challenge: If you are going to find God through His Son, Jesus, then decide that your commitment is to be a *whole-hearted* one. No half measures.

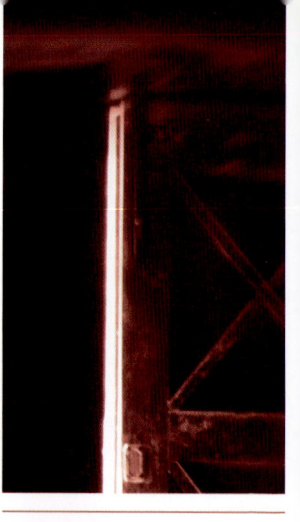

# Open the Door

**STEP 07**

THE **SEVENTH AND FINAL STEP** TO FINDING GOD IS: *receive Jesus Christ into your life as your Lord and Saviour.* This is what Christ said to some people in the very last book of the Bible: 'Here I am! I stand at the door and knock. If anyone hears my voice and opens the door, I will come in ...' (Revelation 3:20).

Christ is speaking metaphorically here, of course. He uses the image of a door to suggest that at the central part of our personality we have the power to either allow someone to enter our lives, or keep them out. If you are married you did something like this when you said your marriage vows. In an act of commitment you opened the door of your heart to allow another person into your life. Something similar takes place when you surrender your life to Jesus Christ. He stands at the door of your life asking for admittance. He will not force Himself upon you. The door has to be opened from the inside. In other words – you need to *invite* Him in.

So now the greatest moment in your life has come. This is the hour I hope when you are going to make your personal commitment to Jesus Christ. I cannot be entirely sure about this, but I would imagine over the minutes in which you have been reading this booklet, you have been aware of being drawn, perhaps in a way you have never experienced before, to think seriously about God and what He has done for you in Christ. God is very close to you now. All that remains is for you to open the door of your inner life and let Him come in. But how?

# presence

A friend of mine, when describing how he became a Christian, put it this way: 'I got down on my knees and simply said "yes" to Jesus Christ. That "yes" was the opening of the door through which Jesus Christ walked into my life.' Saying 'yes' to Jesus means being willing to make Him Lord and Master over every part of your being.

But pause again on the verge of this momentous decision and be in no doubt about its magnitude. You are not forced to accept; you are still free to say 'no'. Saying 'yes' to Jesus, however, means forgiveness of all your sin, the guarantee of His presence and power in your life while you remain here on earth, and a place in heaven when you die. Does the issue need to be argued any more? I urge you – say 'yes' to Jesus now.

If you would like to surrender your life to Jesus, a special prayer has been prepared to help you do this, which you will find on the next page. Find a quiet spot where you will be uninterrupted, sit or kneel, whichever you prefer, and pray the prayer sincerely and from the bottom of your heart.

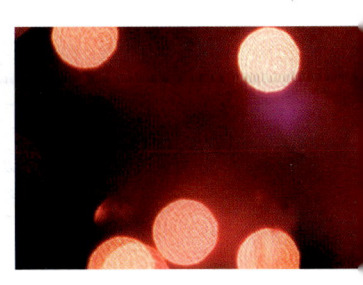

# A Prayer of Commitment

O GOD MY FATHER, THIS IS THE DAY IN WHICH I MAKE MY SURRENDER AND COMMITMENT TO YOU. I make the choice, with all its implications, to receive You into my heart and life today. I have found out how not to live; now I am going to find out how to live – with You.

You sent Your Son into this world to die on a cross so that my sins could be forgiven. I am so grateful for that. I am ready to fling open the doors of my inner being and let You in.

I am sorry that I have resisted You for so long. I repent of my sin and ask You to forgive me for my stubbornness, my independence and for trying to make my life work without You.

I know that as I reach up, You are reaching down. Cleanse me from every sin. Give me the assurance, even now, that You have received me, and put into my heart an unshakeable conviction that I am Yours and You are mine.

Help me from now on to live a life worthy of You. Give me the courage to tell others of my commitment. Guide me through every day so that I know I am no longer on my own. I ask this in and through the name of the Lord Jesus Christ, Your Son, my Saviour. Amen.

---

AS A RECORD OF THE DAY AND HOUR IN WHICH YOU RECEIVED CHRIST, YOU MIGHT LIKE TO COMPLETE THE SENTENCE BELOW FOR THAT PURPOSE. KEEP IT SAFE. IT IS YOUR BIRTH CERTIFICATE INTO GOD'S KINGDOM.

Today, _____ / _____ 20\_\_\_\_ I committed my life to Jesus Christ and received Him into my life as my Saviour and Lord.

Signed _____

# What Happens Next?

ON THESE FINAL PAGES, I WANT TO ANSWER A QUESTION THAT MAY NOW BE UPPERMOST IN YOUR MIND: *what happens next?*

Before I do so, however, let me remind you of what you have done. In committing your life to Jesus Christ you have settled the greatest issue that can ever confront a man or a woman in this world - how to find God and enter into a relationship with Him.

There are several things you can do, however, to help develop the new life that has entered your soul. FIRST, tell someone (such as a close friend) you have become a Christian. They might not understand all the implications of what you have done, but you will be surprised how sharing this commitment with someone will deepen your own awareness of what you have done.

SECONDLY, if you are not attending a Christian church, try to join one as soon as possible. It is extremely important to join with other Christians, as God has asked that we do this (see Hebrews 10:25). If you have no church connections, you might find it helpful to visit a few of the churches in your area before deciding which one you would like to settle in. While all Christian churches believe in God and practise the Christian faith, they have different styles and forms of worship. Find one you are comfortable with and then talk to the minister or leader and tell him you have recently committed yourself to Christ.

THIRDLY, plan to spend some time every day (or at least regularly) in reading the Bible and talking to God in prayer. These are vitally important spiritual exercises that will help you to grow and develop as a Christian. God bless you in your daily walk with the Lord Jesus Christ.

*If you have prayed the Prayer of Commitment on page 30, we would love to hear from you.*
*Write to CWR, Waverley Abbey House,*
*Waverley Lane, Farnham, Surrey GU9 8EP, UK*
*or email mail@cwr.org.uk*
*You may like to know of a booklet Selwyn wrote for new Christians, Every Day with Jesus for New Christians, available direct from CWR (www.cwrstore.org.uk) or your local Christian bookshop. With two months of suggested daily Bible readings and comment from Selwyn, it will help you to develop your newfound relationship with God.*